CAMP

Living a Life of Clarity, Alignment, Manifestation,
and Positive Impact

Ivory J. Hunter

WakeRight Publishing

LOS ANGELES, CALIFORNIA

Ivory J. Hunter/WakeRight Publishing

CAMP: Living a Life of Clarity, Alignment, Manifestation, and Positive Impact/ Ivory J. Hunter. -- 1st ed.
ISBN 978-1-7336276-3-4

CONTENTS

INTRODUCTION

Growing up as a Christian I developed a relationship with God and a keen understanding of faith and unconditional love. However, because of certain (man-made) Christian principles and beliefs, I also developed some confusion and fear. Before we move any further: this is not about bashing religion at all; it's about sharing my journey and what led me to my beliefs. Religion is beautiful, but in some ways, it can be divisive and a tad bit arrogant. Most religions feel like their way is the "only truth" and the only way! I humbly disagree. We were not created to be divided and torn apart. We were created from Love, in order to love, and unite. That said, religion is also incredibly important, because it allows people the opportunity to connect with, and have faith in something higher than self. Without connection and awareness of a higher source—to each that source is different, to some it's God and to others it's simply a cause greater than ourselves—I'm afraid of what this world would be. Scary to even imagine a world without faith, without love, without accountability.

Throughout this book I am going to try my best to always focus on the positive, because I believe in the "Law of Attraction." Whatever we focus on gains momentum and grows. My focus will be on light and love because that's what I want to see grown and that's what the world needs more of.

So why did I decide to write this book?

My purpose in life is to love, inspire, and encourage people. I want to share what I have been learning and what I humbly believe to be the secret to a happy, purposeful life. I am a self-proclaimed student of life who has failed so many times; and every failure is just an opportunity to learn when you have a healthy mindset about it. I want to share information that can help change lives, break negative cycles, and ultimately promote happiness, and increase love and self-awareness. I know this mindset works because I have applied it to my own life from raising my daughters, by counseling friends and family, and by teaching and training students. Applying a healthy mindset and perspective has always led to positive results.

I have had a very blessed life thus far because I've always had a grateful mindset. I attribute that to my upbringing. I come from a huge family with a foundation of love on both sides. I'm so grateful for my family because they have taught me everything I needed to know in order to navigate my way through my human experience. I've learned from the good and the bad.

My dad used to tell me often that he didn't want me to be like him—he wanted me to be better than him. He passed away (transitioned) at the young age of forty-four. He had a lot of demons that he couldn't overcome; which is another reason I've written this book. I don't want people to have to suffer in this lifetime because they are holding on to the past and blaming other people for their situations.

People don't do anything to us. We put out a vibration and people jump on it. In one of the later chapters I will discuss how to manage your vibration and energy. We are the creators of our own realities; we can choose the thoughts that we think and get the results that we expect. My father blamed his father for his shortcomings in life, which was unhealthy. Many people live this way and it prevents them from living the life they deserve.

My parents had me when they graduated high school. They were both only eighteen years old. At that point my grandfather gave my father an ultimatum. He told my dad that he could go to college on a basketball scholarship while my mother and I stayed with him (my grandfather), or that he could take care of his family by himself. My dad wasn't having any of that; he wanted to do it "my way" just like Frank Sinatra. Consequently, he joined the United States Air Force and took me and my mother with him. After my dad finished the military, we moved back to Bristol, Pennsylvania where I was born. He was still a young man, then in his early twenties, dealing with a lot of issues and resistance when we moved back. His biggest problem—

playing the blame game and not taking responsibility for his actions.

My dad was smart, charismatic, benevolent, talented, funny, and loving. He was also unfaithful, verbally and physically abusive, and struggled with drug addiction. He was a complicated person but a loving father and deep down a good person. I loved him unconditionally because I understood where his anger stemmed from. He didn't just turn out that way just because he wanted to have a hard life. His behavior stemmed from the strict manner in which my grandfather raised him.

My grandfather was old school; he believed in hard work and discipline because he was a self-made man and incredibly successful despite having no education. He was seventeen years old when he married my grandmother and moved from Florida to Pennsylvania after they gave birth to my father. He was never taught how to be a man, how to be a husband, or how to be a father. He learned everything on his own because he was determined to succeed no matter what. My grandfather used to always say, "Do whatever you need to do to obtain your objective," and that's how he lived his life. No doubt my grandfather made a lot of mistakes as a father and husband. He was verbally and physically abusive with my father. Not because he didn't love my dad; he thought he was making my dad stronger and better. My grandfather was ignorant—I didn't say stupid; he simply wasn't equipped with the proper tools and I believe he did the best he could with the information he had. He wasn't terribly self-aware and his emotional I.Q.

was probably on the lower end. Consequently, my dad never felt loved by my grandfather and spent most of his adult life butting heads with him.

My grandmother who we called Big Mot was the total opposite of my grandfather; she always represented unconditional love and compassion. Because of her, my dad experienced a great sense of love growing up and her affection and devotion to her son continued all of his life. Essentially my dad had a choice regarding the type of life he wanted to create for himself because he had parents who were polar opposites in how they showed love. Our imprints, or our earliest experiences as young people, are an important factor in our behavior growing up and for many their entire lives. Whatever we focus on is what we give energy and power to. My dad focused on what he perceived as a "lack of love" from my grandfather, and as a result that imprint haunted him all of his life. He didn't create or hone the proper tools to "break the cycle." He didn't have the tools to let go of the resistance (blame), and as such he didn't live a life of peace, understanding, and self-knowledge. My goal in this book is to share my journey and show people an array of tools that they need to let go of the resistance and live a life of Clarity, Alignment, Manifestation, in order to have a Positive impact on others—how to live a life of CAMP.

CHAPTER ONE

CLARITY

Meaning of Clarity, as defined by Merriam-Webster Dictionary:

Clarity- (n) The quality of being clear, in particular. The quality of coherence and intelligibility.

<u>Several Synonyms</u>- accuracy, brightness, certainty, directness, exactness, transparency, precision,

<u>Several Antonyms-</u> cloudiness, fogginess, haziness, mistiness, dimness, vagueness, muddiness

Growing up as a child I was raised by my extraordinary and loving mother Maria. She raised me and my younger brother Bobby all by herself. She and my dad got divorced when I was very young, because my dad couldn't stay faithful and because he was verbally and physically abusive. I give my mother so much respect and credit because she did whatever she had to do in order to make sure my brother and I never went without. She has always been extremely loving and forgiving. In spite of the hell that my father put her through, she never bashed him to my brother and me because she knew how much we loved him and how important it was for us to have a relationship with him.

My father was a large man; 6'2" and at least 250 pounds which made it traumatic as a child to witness your mother being cursed at or hit. I tried to block it out, but it was always scary as a child to witness and experience any kind of abuse. It was also confusing to me because my father was my hero. How could he snap like that at any given moment and turn into a monster? It didn't make sense because there were times when he was the best person to be around. He was funny, loving, he took great pleasure in cooking for his family and friends, and he was always the life of the party. I loved going everywhere with my dad. He would put me on his shoulders and I felt like I was on top of the world.

Unfortunately my dad truly took me "everywhere" with him—he even took me with him when he would cheat on my mother. Can you imagine how broken an individual must be to expose their children to such destructive behavior? Fortunately for me, I got to witness the polarity in a person who was my hero. He was always so transparent with me, sometimes to a fault. However, I will always remember him saying to me, "I don't want you to be like me; I want you to be better than me." My dad loved me so much and I felt it, even after all of the things I witnessed.

Loving my father regardless of what I experienced was one of the first *Moments of Clarity* in my life. It taught me and gave me Clarity to love unconditionally. Seeing the beauty and the beast inside my father—and understanding where it came from—taught me to love unconditionally and look past a person's actions. I know now that most people are broken, and that destructive behavior is learned behavior. Hurt people, hurt people. As a result, that understanding of human behavior allowed me to connect with people from different backgrounds and embrace and accept everyone without judgement. Of course people will argue that everyone judges to a certain extent, and that may be true. However, when we are self-aware and compassionate we will try our best not to be judgmental.

We all have had, and will continue to have, *Moments of Clarity* in our lives. It is a wise choice to be intentional and deliberate when it comes to seeking clarity in our lives.

CAMP REFLECTIONS

Can you remember your first Moment of Clarity in your life? What was it and what did you learn and how did you feel?

_____

_____

_____

_____

_____

_____

_____

_____

_____

_____

_____

_____

_____

_____

_____

_____

_____

_____

_____

_____

PURPOSE OF CLARITY

Why is it so important to have clarity in your life? What is the purpose? Let's first take a look at some of the antonyms mentioned at the beginning of this chapter. Cloudiness, fogginess, haziness, mistiness, dimness, vagueness, and muddiness. All of those words ending in "ness" will make your life a complete mess.

Clarity is important on all levels in order to make decisions, to chase dreams, or to pursue whatever it is you desire. Without clarity we don't have vision or purpose and without vision or purpose we are just existing and taking up space. Who wants to just exist? Forget that mindset! Take advantage of this beautiful opportunity to live an impactful life during your experience on this Earth.

The purpose of clarity is to help you succeed in whatever you're attempting to accomplish. When we our intentional about our direction it defines what we do every day. Clarifying not only our purpose but our direction reinforces our ultimate life purpose. When we aren't clear about a goal, it's nearly impossible to achieve it. When we don't know *why* we should do something, we will never be committed to taking action. Napoleon Hill once said, "There is one quality that one must possess to win, and that is passion, purpose, the knowledge of what one wants, and burning desire to possess it."

People who constantly have a desire to achieve something meaningful in life have a strong thirst for clarity. It's the solution to reach deeper into ourselves; to find out what makes us come alive. Everyone starts from a place of uncertainty because we all have a variety of aptitudes, interests, and frames of reference from our life experiences. But once our purpose is defined, we become invincible. It is important to, "know your why." Knowing your "why" is an important first step in figuring out how to achieve the goals that excite you and to create a life you love rather than getting through each day and merely existing. People who are successful have clarity. They have a clear understanding of what success means to them, and everything that they do is aligned with their goals. Their daily actions are consistent and clear and it keeps them on target with their goals. According to Deepak Chopra, M.D. founder of The Chopra Foundation, what most people find when they look at themselves are:

- *Confusion*: this manifests as not setting clear priorities because the path ahead doesn't look clear and decisive.

- *Distraction:* this manifests as a multitude of small things that pull your attention in multiple directions.

- *Disorganization*: this manifests as a lack of orderly thinking that leads to unproductive results.

Most people's lives are not crystal clear—not even close. The struggle is real and most adults self-defined purpose for living is murky at best. So don't feel bad if you're not clear on your purpose, because I will discuss how to gain clarity a little later on.

Millions of people have no clarity or purpose or any idea how to obtain it. You will no longer be in that sinking ship once you make the decision to change your mindset. Everything in life is about mindset. Self-discovery and self-awareness will always be a part of our journey—there's no shortcut or way around it.

It's important to stay present while on our journey at all times, because the Universe is always working to bring us clarity. If we are stressed, worried, negative, or distracted by our thoughts; we will constantly miss the opportunities that are in front of us on a daily basis. Stay up, stay on point, and get out of your head as much as possible. Guard your thoughts and manage your thoughts, because our thoughts lead to our actions. I have been studying Abraham Hicks for some time now, and she always talks about activating new thoughts. She says, "We can't deactivate a thought; we can only activate a new thought." Thoughts turn into existence in the absence of resistance. If you're conscious of your thoughts you have a way better chance of gaining clarity in any situation. Be the observer of your thoughts; because you're not your thoughts.

CAMP REFLECTIONS

Why do you think having Clarity in your life can be beneficial to you and those around you?

_____

_____

_____

_____

_____

_____

_____

_____

_____

_____

_____

_____

_____

_____

_____

HOW TO GAIN CLARITY

If don't have clarity in our lives, we will be constantly reacting to life instead of creating the lives that we desire and deserve. When you are clear about what gives you joy and makes you loving, happy, and healthy; you can have joy, be loving, happy, and healthy. Picture a life with less stress, less confusion, and less doubt. Clarity allows us to navigate through life easier, but gaining clarity entails self-awareness, change, and dedication to becoming a better you.

If it's your desire to make healthier decisions, become more dependable, accomplish goals, be healthier and live an impactful life; these six strategies will help you gain greater clarity.

1. **Remove the Clutter -** You can't operate in life thoroughly and efficiently if you're unorganized. You need to create space in both the physical and the mental aspects of your life. You can't work effectively or live diligently while in a state of chaos. Make sure you meditate daily and keep your living and work environment cleaned and organized.

2. **Pinpoint What Matters -** Identify what you are passionate about in all areas of your life. Make sure that you write down what you want for your work and personal life. Write down your ideal relationship and

what it looks and feels like. If you want to start a new business, you have to put it on paper first. There's something about seeing your thoughts on paper. It gives it life. Thoughts turn into action. Whatever you are passionate about; make sure you write it down.

3. **Clean House** - It is super important to make sure you alleviate all distractions and stay focused. You must protect your energy and pay attention to what you're tuned into and the people you're surrounding yourself with. You are the company you keep. Staying positive and focused is going to be key, so you must eliminate distractions. Lose or mitigate unhealthy habits and stop hanging around people who don't add value to your life.

4. **Focus on One Thing** - I'm sure you have multiple desires and goals that you are going to eventually accomplish. However, it is important to focus your energy on the one project or goal you want to manifest. If you spread yourself too thin you won't be able to give the tasks to complete your goals the proper energy in order to enjoy the success you desire. When this one thing manifests, you will have the means to facilitate the rest of your desires and goals.

5. **Be a Beast** - Take care of your physical health. What good is it to work smart to achieve your desires and be unhealthy? Be proactive so you don't have to be reactive. Eat well and exercise. Let go of the sugars and the excessive snacking. Make healthier eating

choices for yourself. Take care of your body and your body will take care of you. Make it a habit to do some form of exercise or movement every day. Consistency unlocks discipline which then produces positive results.

6. **Meditate Twice a Day** - My grandmother Big Mot asked me one day to explain to her what it meant to meditate. I told her that when we pray, we are asking God for something, and when we meditate, we are quieting our minds and listening to God. So make sure that you learn to meditate and get quiet so you can put yourself in a receptive space to receive clarity.

CAMP REFLECTIONS

What are some of the tools that you are going to use to gain clarity in your life? What will be your Daily Routine? (Be deliberate and specific)

_____

_____

_____

_____

_____

_____

_____

_____

_____

_____

_____

_____
_____
_____
_____
_____
_____
_____
_____
_____

EXAMPLE OF CLARITY

It was September 2018 when I received some news that would soon put me in a bad financial situation. In 2016, I created a relationship app and was blessed to get an angel investor to finance the project. He was the perfect investor because he was all in, supporting me and my vision for the app. Things were going great; I had an amazing flow going on in my life at the time. He made sure I had a basic salary to cover all of my necessities and to take care of my three daughters Mariah, Sienna, and Olivia while I worked on developing the app.

Being a single father raising three daughters in Los Angeles isn't cheap or easy; so I learned how to operate on a tight budget. However; it was blessing in disguise not to have the extra financial resources to do the things I wanted to do with my daughters. It allowed me to be present and spend more creative and meaningful time bonding with them.

Pro-tip: Part of being on the "leading edge" is being aware of the purpose behind your current experience or situation and to gain understanding and clarity in real time. A lot of people look back after the fact and understand why they had those experiences in the past and only find purpose then. The key is being present so you can gain clarity and learn your lessons quicker.

I was proud of the fact that I worked hard to rebuild my credit, and I was feeling confident that I would make massive amounts of money to eventually pay back all of the people who have helped me along my journey. And then there was the day my investor asked to meet with me face to face. We sat down and he looked at me with hurt in his eyes as he told me that he had some personal issues with his finances and was unable to continue to fund me—effective immediately. At that point I had some serious decision making to do. Here I am taking care of these girls all by myself with a car note, insurance, bills, groceries, and credit card debt with no income and very little savings. This is when I had my *Moment of Clarity*.

I knew that I didn't want to REPEAT the SAME FAILURES by borrowing money from anyone to get myself out of this mess that I created for myself. I decided to utilize some of the tools I had in my tool belt in order to move forward and focus on what I wanted as opposed to what I didn't have. I knew I had a lot of tools in my tool belt because for years I had always surrounded myself with people smarter and wiser than me so that I could learn and grow. I've always read inspirational books and listened to motivational speakers to enhance my knowledge and awareness. Furthermore, the past several years I had started listening to Abraham Hicks daily and it shifted my perspective on life and it had been easier ever since.

For that I'm grateful. The teachings of Abraham Hicks have gave me an understanding of who I truly am. It has also increased my faith to a deeper level of understanding and awareness. I also have an overwhelming sense of trust (rather than fear) in what I don't know. What was the tool I utilized?

I decided to IGNORE MY CURRENT REALITY and create the reality that I wanted. But what did that mean for me? It meant that I had to ignore the bill collectors, accept that my credit score was going to drop again, and FOCUS ON FEELING GOOD while I trusted things would work out for me, because they always do.

Pro-tip: One of your mantras needs to be, "Things are always working out for me," because they are. If you look back on everything that you've already stressed about and been through you eventually got past it. You may not have always liked or accepted your results but things truly always work out for us.

Focusing myself toward feeling good was important, because my energy had to be positive if I wanted things to continue to work out for me. I couldn't block it with my own resistance by worrying or stressing. Energy carries momentum and I wanted to make sure that I put out positive energy and create forward momentum for myself. So I decided to write a book and it all began to unfold in a wonderful way. I decided to call my first book, *Waking Up With The Right Mindset—50 Positive Thoughts To Start Your Day*. It was how I lived my life so I decided to write a book about it! Clarity!

CAMP REFLECTION

Have you had another moment of Clarity so far since reading? If so, what is it? What do you plan on doing about it? (Write it down so you can see it and visualize it.)

_____

_____

_____

_____

_____

_____

_____

_____

_____

_____

_____

_____

_____

_____

_____

CHAPTER TWO

ALIGNMENT

Meaning of Alignment:

Alignment- (n) the act of aligning or state of being aligned.

Some Synonyms- adjustment, calibration, arrangement, order, positioning

Some Antonyms- nonalignment, nonalignment.

Nothing is more important than your alignment, because it's really the only thing that you can control. It has to be at the top of your list daily because we teach life how to treat us. We are either teaching the universe to create positive experiences for us or to deliver negative experiences. The reality that you live now, including the things you love along with the problems and struggles, are what you have taught the universe to create for you based off of your alignment. The universe gives you what you request based on your thoughts, feelings, and emotions. We cannot lie to the Universe because it's not listening to what we say, it's listening to how we feel and think. I have recently discovered why I have struggled so much financially in my life. Thinking back on some of my imprints, I can recall how I would hear my grandmother Juanita talk about her dreams in front of our family. She was my hero because she had the biggest heart in the world; she was talented and fearless. However, she didn't have support because certain members of her family would ridicule her and tell her that she wasn't going to make it. It never stopped her from pursuing her dreams though. She dreamed all the way up until she transitioned on April 29, 2019 at eighty-five years old. Sadly enough she never accomplished her dreams; because the seeds that were planted in her subconsciously somehow made her believe that she would never make it. That is why it's important to make sure that your expectations match your desires if you want to them to happen.

So, how did my grandmother's experience affect my financial instability? It's simple to explain; but may be a little more difficult to understand. Those seeds of doubt were also planted in me by witnessing my grandmother's dreams constantly marginalized and belittled. I, too, have been a dreamer all of my life because I wanted so badly to make it big, so I could take care of my grandmother and help facilitate her dreams. She was my WHY. However, it wasn't until recently that I discovered I wasn't aligned with my desires. I self-sabotaged because subconsciously I didn't believe I would truly achieve my dreams. Failures, doubt, false beliefs, and other people's opinions can and will affect your outcome. That's why it is important that you put your alignment first and be aware at all times of the quality of your thoughts and how you're feeling. The key is to become more conscious about what you're teaching the universe about who you are now because who you are now is what's important. You don't have to fight circumstances if you desire a change. You just have to change your thoughts and beliefs about it. Align your thoughts and feelings with what you desire.

CAMP REFLECTION

Do you have any dreams or desires that have yet to be fulfilled? If so, what are they? Why do you think you haven't accomplished them yet?

_____

_____

_____

_____

_____

_____

_____

_____

_____

_____

_____

_____

_____

_____

_____

_____

PURPOSE OF ALIGNMENT

A great friend of mine, Thom, once told me that it doesn't matter how strong a train is or how many engines it has pulling it. If it isn't on the track, that bad boy isn't going anywhere, no matter how bad you want it to. I love that metaphor because it's the same concept regarding our own alignment. If we aren't truly aligned with our desires; they will never happen no matter how hard we try. Effort is important but your alignment with what you desire is truly the key.

Our focus on "what is" or what we call our current situation doesn't help us when things aren't going well for us. When things happen; we have two vibrations that encompass the "what is." They are the circumstances of our reality and the feelings we have about it. This is where understanding your alignment plays a key factor in your circumstances changing for the better. Remember the universe doesn't listen to what you say, it's responding to how you feel. So understanding the purpose of your alignment is important if you want to shift circumstances. You have to change how you feel about the situation in order to change your reality.

I remember for years I struggled with being faithful to women. I constantly kept repeating the same failures by unintentionally hurting women. Not because I was a mean person set out to hurt women. It was the fact that I wasn't aligned and continued to keep the cycle going by cheating and having multiple women—the actions I witnessed from my father and grandfather. It's not right and I'm not proud of it, but it was an imprint that I allowed to shape me. I have had some incredible women in my life, and I have sabotaged many of those relationships because I wasn't aligned or conscious. I realized that subconsciously I didn't feel like I could have a successful relationship or deserve to be in one. I didn't trust people because I didn't trust myself. The purpose of alignment is truly about changing your perspective to see things, people, and situations the way God does. It's about aligning up with your inner being, which is God (Source Energy).

We are all a part of and made up of Source Energy. When you are in alignment with who you really are you change your perspective and change your reality. Without alignment it's impossible to have clarity. Once I made it my goal to put my alignment first my whole reality changed. I became more transparent with women and everyone else in my life. There's freedom in transparency, and it gives other people the permission to be vulnerable and transparent. Being aligned makes you more conscious and you hold yourself more accountable for your actions.

Selfishly I would tell women that I didn't want to be in a relationship to sometimes scare them away. That didn't work because most of them would still decide that it was okay to just mess around without commitment. Or they would feel like they could be the one who changed me. People let me be clear with you; people change because they want to change. You can't make a person change. Unfortunately, that was always enough for me to pursue that type of relationship with them even though I already knew that they would eventually catch feelings and get hurt. It was easy for me to repeat that pattern for so long and justify my behavior because I was treating them nicely and I was honest at the start. However, there was no way I could continue to hurt women once I became aligned. I knew deep down that even though they said that they could handle a relationship without commitment, they ultimately wanted more. So I couldn't continue making those unhealthy decisions knowing that it was wrong. Choose unconditional alignment because the moment you choose a better feeling, circumstances shift.

CAMP REFLECTIONS

What have been some of the things you struggled with because you weren't aligned? How could those situations have turned out differently?

_____

_____

_____

_____

_____

_____

_____

_____

_____

_____

_____

_____

_____

_____

_____

_____

_____

_____

_____

_____

HOW TO GAIN ALIGNMENT

If you want to successfully manifest the life you desire, it is essential to focus yourself into alignment with God (Source Energy), because we are all an extension of Source Energy. We are much more powerful when we are aligned. It is always important to try your best to focus yourself into feeling good, because when you are, you are a vibrational match with the things you desire. You have to be committed to maintaining your alignment because it is the way that you create your reality. There will be challenges because things are going to happen daily that are out of our control. In addition to the daily challenges, it takes time to unlearn and retrain ourselves from all of the negative conditioning we have endured throughout the years. The good news is that it can be done—all you have to do is choose to focus yourself into feeling good and live the life that you desire.

It's going to take consistency with having inspired action to stay aligned, and constant work at becoming the best version of yourself. Consistent practice will make you become effective at creating the life that you want and deserve and truly change your perspective on everything in.

To practice staying in alignment try following these 7 steps:

1. **Meditation** - Meditation isn't about becoming a different person, a new person, or even a better person. It's about training in awareness and getting clearer perspective. You're not trying to turn off your thoughts or feelings. You're learning to observe them without judgement. Eventually you will begin to understand them as well.

2. **Journal** - Journaling generally involves the practice of keeping a diary or journal that explores thoughts and feelings surrounding your life. There's something about writing it down on paper that gives your thoughts and ideas life, and it's a great source for self-inspiration. Write down your daily affirmations and everything you appreciate. Everything starts with gratitude.

3. **Vision Board** - A vision board is a collage of images, pictures, and affirmations of one's dreams and desires designed to serve as a source of inspiration and motivation, and to use the Law of Attraction to attain goals. Creating this visual representation in constant view is a vivid reminder of what your values and priorities are and to keep you inspired and excited.

4. **Affirmations** - Affirmations are a powerful way to improve your mindset on a daily basis, and research has shown that affirmations can increase our feelings of self-worth. Affirmations are positive reminders or statements that can be used to encourage yourself or others. Daily affirmations have the power to change your life. They are simple messages repeated over and over, and they begin to take root in your mind. They change your thinking which then changes your reality.

5. **Abraham-Hicks Videos** - My favorite way to stay on track is by listening to Abraham Hicks videos every day. I have listened to hundreds of them and I never get bored. I take something from every video I listen to. Listening to Abraham Hicks has been important in my personal growth and in my understanding of the Law of Attraction, as well as changing my whole perspective of life. That works for me but may not work for you. However, it doesn't matter if you're Buddhist, Christian, Muslim, Spiritual, or whatever; just make sure you listen to and take in content on a daily basis from the positive people who teach and inspire you.

6. **Inspirational Books** - Reading inspirational books is a great way to help you focus, grow, and feel good. We attract whatever we focus on, regardless of if it's something we want or don't want. There are so many incredible books to keep you on track and inspired.

You have to learn to keep your focus on track to manifest the life that you desire.

CAMP REFLECTIONS

What are some of the tools that you will apply to your daily life in order to gain alignment?

_____

_____

_____

_____

_____

_____

_____

_____

_____

_____

_____

_____

_____

_____

_____

_____

_____

_____

EXAMPLE OF ALIGNMENT

Once I decided to write the book it was important for me to make sure that I was a vibrational match with what I wanted. This was important because we cannot experience anything that is not in sync with our vibration.

I'll explain this as simply as possible. Everything is made up of energy. The trees are energy, water is energy, you are energy. Everything is energy. Even our thoughts, feelings, and emotions are energy. You are an energetic being and your mood is a direct indicator of your vibration at any given moment.

It was important for me to be able to apply some of my tools in order to stay aligned and be a vibrational match for my desire to complete this book. The first tool that I knew I had to use was my understanding of energy and momentum. Everything starts from gratitude, so I began to be more deliberate every morning with how I woke up and started my day. I am blessed and grateful to take care of my three amazing daughters throughout the week. I started waking up an hour earlier every day in order to take time to align myself. I used to wake up and turn on the news, check social media, check my messages, and emails. That is a recipe for disaster if you're not aligned. We have to be conscious of what we tune into first thing in the morning, because certain things may trigger a negative emotion or feeling. In turn, this will continue to carry on for the rest of your day, because energy has momentum. My routine was consistent and I began to wake up daily and express my gratitude, say my affirmations, meditate, and do push-ups and sit ups. Consistency is the key to becoming disciplined at any area of your life. After I practiced my daily routine I would wake my girls up an extra hour earlier, so that they could wake up and ease into the morning without being rushed. I spent every morning loving on them and showing the universe how grateful I was for them. By focusing on the good first thing in the morning I created more good feeling moments throughout the day.

I'm not going to fabricate and say that it was an easy process because not being able to pay bills and do certain things for my daughters was tough on my ego. However, one thing that I knew for sure was that our current situation doesn't define who we are. It's who we are and how we live that defines us. Whenever negative thoughts come up it's important to catch them early and try to reroute your thoughts. We cannot deactivate a thought, we can only de-emphasize the thought, and activate a new thought.

The more I put my alignment first the more things started to line up and fall in place. My cousin Chuck introduced me to a small publishing company that helped authors facilitate their vision. I found an outstanding graphic artist to incorporate my vision for the cover. The words of the book seemed to flow for me so effortlessly. Meanwhile my bills were piling up, my credit score was dropping drastically, and I owed a great deal of money. A lot of people would've stressed out immensely but I knew that I had to trust the process. Instead of stressing I continued to give love and pour into others. It is so gratifying being able to help others; the more love I put out there, the more love I have been rewarded with. Love is not given in order to get something in return; love is what we are born to do. I can't emphasize enough that everything in life really starts with mindset. I simply decided to change my perspective and as a result I changed my reality and finished my book.

Alignment!

CAMP REFLECTIONS

How has your perspective changed so far about your alignment? How do you think it will benefit you going forward?

_____

_____

_____

_____

_____

_____

_____

_____

_____

_____

_____

_____

_____

_____

_____

_____

_____

_____

_____

CHAPTER THREE

MANIFESTATION

Meaning of Manifestation:

Manifestation- (n) The action or fact of showing an abstract idea.

<u>Some Synonyms-</u> display, demonstration, showing, show, exhibition, sign

<u>Some Antonyms-</u> Concealment, hiding, reality, secret, vagueness, obscurity.

There are numerous definitions of the word, "manifest," but to simplify it, manifestation is something that is put into your physical reality through thoughts, beliefs, and feelings. It's the perfect example of the Law of Attraction at work. Whatever you focus on is what you attract into your reality. To manifest, you focus through meditation, visualization, or by your conscious or subconscious thoughts, feelings, or beliefs.

We attract what we want or don't want. I'll give you examples of both attracting the wanted and unwanted.

One day my good friend Cirroc and I took our daughters to the Getty Museum for an afternoon outing. As soon as we got there I was overly protective of my youngest daughter Olivia. All day I kept reminding my other two daughters Mariah and Sienna to keep an eye on Olivia. Thinking back on that day, I realize that I had way too much fear and worry about something happening. As the day progressed my worrying didn't stop. I kept on top of my daughters to make sure that they kept an extra eye on Olivia. Finally we finished spending the day at the museum, and I felt relieved that nothing happened, and we all had a great time. However, as we got on the elevator to leave Olivia's hand got stuck in the elevator door as it closed. Panic and fear set in for everybody on the elevator except for one gentleman who thankfully kept his cool and figured out how to get her hand out safely. I was so grateful to him, but it was a powerful learning moment for me. I had to realize that I created that situation by placing so much attention on trying to prevent an accident that I attracted exactly what I didn't want.

The Law of Attraction has been working in our lives from the beginning. Most of us aren't aware of it; so happenstances are merely brushed off as coincidences.

Years ago when I had just graduated college and was living up in the Bay Area I was at a mall and came across a calendar of some beautiful women and had to purchase it to take it home. All of the women on the calendar were beautiful; but there was one particular one who stood out to me. Her month was December and in my opinion she was perfect. We even shared the same major in college. She was my dream girl. I kept her month showing on my wall and would look at her every day. She was from St. Louis and I was living in Northern California at the time. Fast forward years two years later and I was living in Los Angeles, California. My cousin Kevin opened up a store on Melrose Avenue and I worked with him. It was a popular urban retail store that catered to athletes and celebrities. One day we had an event with a radio station, and they were bringing in some girls from the calendar that my dream girl was on. I was super excited and hoped that the girl I liked would be one of the four girls who showed up. Unfortunately she wasn't, so I started dating one of the other girls from the calendar. She wasn't my dream girl but she was still pretty great and (unbeknownst to me at the time) I was able to manifest dating a girl from my calendar. It seemed like a coincidence, but was the Law of Attraction trying to bring me nearer to my desires?

About a year later, I took a walk to the bank near my house, and I ran into the girl from the calendar who I liked and looked at everyday on my wall. It was unimaginable to me at the time, and I couldn't believe that I was seeing her face to face. We met, but nothing happened except for my excitement at seeing my dream girl face to face. Was that a coincidence? Or was this the Law of Attraction bringing me someone I desired and looked at every day?

At that time I had never heard of the Law of Attraction, so it was pure coincidence to me. The following year I got into a relationship with an incredible girl who lived in San Diego. I really loved her and enjoyed being with her. She treated me and the people close to me very well. I thought I had finally grown up and found the right person for me who made me better. However, one day I was out in Los Angeles at a nightclub with my friends having a great time listening to a popular local band called the Polyester Players. I ran into the calendar girl again, and this time we hit it off and connected. I felt bad because I was in a relationship with a beautiful person who I didn't want to hurt. But at that time in my life I was still not conscious or healed of the cycle of hurting women.

Consequently, I found myself in a difficult situation, and I couldn't resist. I led two lives for a few months and I began to see the calendar girl while I still had my girlfriend in San Diego. I felt horrible and guilty as heck because I was lying to two women who I cared about. After a few months it was clear to me that I was in love with the calendar girl. So I decided to end it with my girlfriend in San Diego because I had to follow my heart, and I couldn't deceive her anymore. That was hard to do but how could I ignore my feelings for my dream girl? That type of thing didn't happen to regular people in my mind. I believed that could only happen to celebrities and rich people. Was this a coincidence or was this the Law of Attraction giving me what I wanted?

CAMP REFLECTIONS

Can you remember any times when you were able to manifest something in your life? Have you thought of someone and then they called or texted? Write down the moments that you remember manifesting.

_____

_____

_____

_____

_____

_____

_____

_____

_____

_____

_____

_____

_____

_____

_____

_____

_____

_____

_____

_____

_____

_____

_____

_____

_____

_____

PURPOSE OF MANIFESTATION

I've come to learn that we can change any situation by a conscious decision. Manifestation occurs with the power of a decision. Abraham Hicks says, "Thoughts turn into things in the absence of resistance." When we make up our mind and say: *I want something no matter what*, magic happens and that's the true power that we have to manifest.

We get what we want and we get what we don't, and if you're fed up with getting what you don't want, then it's time to make unconscious manifestations become conscious and intentional. We are all part of the Divine plan and have a specific and important life purpose that we came here to fulfill. This brings me back to one of my favorite quotes by Dr. Wayne Dyer that changed my life. He said that, "we are not human beings having spiritual experiences; we are spiritual beings having human experiences." We came to planet earth to have a human experience with a purpose, so it makes sense that the Universe supports us in fulfilling our purpose. So all of your ideas and the vision that you have are a part of the collective consciousness that make up the universe and allows it to continuously expand.

Sometimes we might be led down a road that takes us to an outcome that our conscious self didn't know we wanted or needed. The Universe always takes us on the scenic path because it's more fulfilling than going the quickest most direct path. Essentially the Universe would like us to drive across country as opposed to flying, so we can truly enjoy the journey and learn along the way. Put another way, the Universe provides us with friction (even if we label that friction as painful or an annoyance). Because we have free will, the Universe lets us choose whether to allow the friction to slow us down or to use the friction to launch us further and faster along the path we are supposed to be on and in the direction of our dreams and true purpose. Our manifestation is linked to our purpose, and some things may manifest quickly, while other things may take years. If things haven't manifested for you yet don't get frustrated. It simply means that you're not yet a vibrational match for whatever it is that you desire.

We all need to realize that whether we believe it or not, sooner or later we receive what we put out into the universe. This is why we need to manifest all of our desires, small or large, practical or impractical. Whatever you desire in this life can be yours. I don't care if it's your career, your significant other, or something material. You need to speak it out loud into existence, write it down, put it on a vision board; just do whatever it takes to see your goals and not block them with your own doubt and false beliefs. Don't manifest your fears and insecurities, manifest your heart's truest desires.

Keep in mind that we're constantly manifesting, because every thought we think creates energy that attracts its likeness. So if you're thinking that things never work out for you, you attract more unpleasant experiences where things don't work out for you. Being aware of this energy flow is key, and you should constantly work to have good feeling thoughts, so you manifest more good positive experiences and results in your life.

CAMP REFLECTIONS

How do you think being intentional about your life will affect you? What are some things you would like to see manifest in your life?

_____

_____

_____

_____

_____

_____

_____

_____

_____

_____

_____

_____

_____

_____

_____

_____

_____

HOW TO MANIFEST

We are more powerful than we know, and we have the ability to manifest and create the realities that we desire.

However, statistics show that the average person has about 70,000 unconscious thoughts per day, and about 80% of them are negative. With that being said, we have to work to rebuild those mental muscles, because we have so much history of negative experiences that are embedded in us from our lives' experiences. It doesn't happen overnight but we have to really train ourselves as much as possible to stay positive and focus on the good. Try these seven steps to help you manifest your desires:

1. **Be Crystal Clear on What You Want** - In order to take the proper steps toward intentional manifestations, you have to know precisely what it is that you want. You must know exactly what you want down to every last detail. If you want a spouse, make sure you are very specific. If you're not specific the Universe may send you a spouse, but they may not quite be the one you truly desire. Be very detailed with everything from the physical and mental attributes of your future mate. Make a list of everything you want and write it down. Be sure to stay positive and focus on what you want as opposed to what you don't want.

2. **Ask God** - The Universe is here to help us but we have to ask in order to receive what we want. Once the Universe is clear on what you want, the manifestation process can occur. Regardless of whether or not we ask, manifestations are going to happen anyway. So rather than leave things for chance, it makes more since to be clear on what you want and ask. In the Bible it says, "Ask and it shall be given to you."

Wake up daily with gratitude, and you can make your desires a part of your daily affirmations that you express to the Universe.

3. **Put In the Work** - Manifesting allows us the ability to co-create with the Universe. We came here to planet Earth to co-create and experience. When we are creating and working toward our goals and desires, it's an awesome part of the journey that enhances our opportunity to manifest. It's time to take action and write down your goals and start working toward whatever it is that you want.

4. **Trust and Allow** - It is so important to trust the process and be willing to accept the results. The road will be as easy as you allow it to be, or as difficult as you make it. In order to manifest, you must trust the process regardless of how tough things may get. When you start questioning the Universe, you keep yourself stuck or sometimes you even go backwards. You have to know that things are always working out for you.

5. **Stay Present to Receive** - The Universe is constantly sending us signs and messages, but often we are caught up in our thoughts, and end up missing messages. We have so many moments of synchronicity when we are aligned and present. The Universe is constantly communicating with us through people, numbers, and signs. We just have to make sure to stay present as much as possible to receive. Be intentional and watch how many times throughout the day

that the Universe is communicating with you in different ways.

6. **Keep Pure Positive Energy** - The Law of Attraction states that we attract what we are sending out. To attract more of the positive things that we want we must raise our vibration. Picture Vibrations as little radio signals that we are constantly sending out into the Universe. We must tune our signal to a very high positive, high vibration in order to receive it back. It all starts with gratitude. Oprah Winfrey once said that the more she expressed her gratitude; the more bountiful positive things came back in return. The key is truly spending time doing things that you love and make you feel good.

7. **Alleviate Resistance** - The reason why people don't manifest their desires, is because of resistance. Resistance comes in many forms, and often times it is an act of self-sabotaging. It can be doubt, fears, false beliefs, hurt, pain, regrets, anger, or blame. These things are understandable because we have a lifetime of experiences and imprints that have shaped us into these thought patterns, both conscious and sub-conscious. Acknowledge when resistance comes up, and work to change your thoughts, feelings, or actions.

CAMP REFLECTIONS

How will you put yourself in a better position to become deliberate at manifesting the things that you desire?

_____

_____

_____

_____

_____

_____

_____

_____

_____

_____

_____

_____

_____

_____

_____

_____

_____

_____

_____

EXAMPLE OF MANIFESTATION

January 16, 2019 is a day that I will never forget, because it was the day that I held the first copy of _Waking up With the Right Mindset—50 Positive Thoughts to Start Your Day_, in my hand. I wasn't looking for confirmation from the Universe, but I have to admit that it felt incredible to see proof on how the Universe operates. It proved to me that thoughts do turn into things in the absence of resistance. I had zero resistance during the writing process because I knew that I wasn't going to let anything or anyone stop me from completing this process. The biggest person I had to worry about was myself. I understood that I couldn't self-sabotage the process with my own actions, or sub-conscious or conscious false beliefs and doubt.

In the past I would get anxious and disappointed when things wouldn't happen fast enough. As a result, I kept things from happening because I wasn't a vibrational match for the things I desired. I would self-sabotage things by my lack of faith, and false beliefs, so things just didn't work out. I used to have regrets about certain things that I wanted that didn't manifest. That was until I understood that the Universe was protecting me from myself. If I would've experienced financial success before I was ready I would've wasted all of my blessings. I was too irresponsible with the choices I made in my life regarding finances and women, so I wasn't ready.

However, as I sat there holding my book for the first time I knew that I was a vibrational match and I was truly ready to handle the fruits of my conscious manifestations.

I put in the work that it took to get myself ready for the things that I desired. I had to be deliberate about allowing things to unfold for me without blocking them. That meant being conscious of my thoughts, feelings, and actions. It took me being consistent because I had to become more disciplined. Lack of discipline has always been something that I allowed to prevent me from achieving my goals. Consistency is what unlocks discipline. If you want a better life then the best thing to do is to make small, incremental changes on a daily basis. With that in mind, you have to be inspired and push yourself to change your habits.

I wouldn't have completed the book if I didn't put my alignment first by being consistent and constantly working to stay aligned. It is so important to put your alignment first if you want to accomplish anything. It is so easy to get distracted if you don't protect your energy. Staying focused was key for me during this process; I knew that I couldn't let anything distract me from my goal of completing the book. As hard as the process was to ignore my debt and bill collectors, writing and completing the book kept me distracted from those pressures. I had to constantly repeat my mantra: "things are always working out for me." I have learned through the process about the power of decision. It taught me to understand that we have the ability to change any situation by making a conscious decision. We have to fully commit and tell ourselves that we want this no matter what. That's when the magic happens and when we manifest our desires. Manifestation!

CAMP REFLECTIONS

Write down ten things that you desire in your life that you WILL manifest. (You have to believe it to see it.)

_____

_____

_____

_____

_____

CHAPTER FOUR

POSITIVE IMPACT

Meaning of Positive Impact:

Positive Impact-Your purpose usually involves some aspect of turning your "mess into a message," or using what you've learned (often the hard way) as a means of being of service to others.

Some Synonyms of Impact- affect, impress, influence, move, reach, strike, sway

Some Antonyms of Positive- harmful, bad, adverse, detrimental, unfavorable

People with a purpose-driven life are focused, dedicated, and committed to making the most of their human experience by positively impacting the lives of others. Making a choice to have impact on the world around you in a positive way is one of the most rewarding experiences. I always knew from an early age that my purpose was bigger than me. My imprint for giving was very strong because I grew up with such loving parents, grandparents, and family members. My childhood memories were filled with so many moments witnessing my family go above and beyond to help others.

Making a choice to place your stamp on the world in a positive way is powerful goal. One of the best ways to find fulfillment, joy, your purpose, and a sense of belonging is to make an effort to improve the lives of others. As I think back on my own personal journey I'm so fortunate to have had so many people pour into me and make a positive impact in my life. It's the people with great hearts who do good deeds that make biggest impact in the world.

There's no singular rule on defining how you make a positive impact on others. You can be a teacher and impact the lives of your students, you can be a parent and impact the lives of your children, you can help out homeless people, you can mentor children— there are so many ways to make a positive impact on others. It just takes the willingness to do so with an open heart.

Staying present is also important because every interaction we have is an opportunity to make a positive impact on others. I love people and have a strong desire to make a positive impact on the world. I truly believe that our lives have purpose, our stories are important, our voices matter, our dreams matter, and we were born to make a positive impact in the world. Each one of us has the ability to make a positive impact on others. It's just a matter of making the most out of doing what you can do with what you have.

Our success is not validated by the amount of money that we obtain or the positions that we hold. What matters is how we use the resources that we have to help others. Money and positions can be taking for granted or abused but they also can be used to make an incredible impact on the world. No matter how irrelevant you may feel your presence in the world makes a big difference. Simple kindness can go a long way by trying to see the best in others when they can't see it in themselves. When we spread love and kindness toward others, it not only raises their vibration, but it replenishes us and helps us raise our own vibration while giving us peace and inner happiness.

There is a woman who was born in 1954 who has become a self-made billionaire, hero, and mega star. Her name is Oprah Winfrey. Ever since she was eleven years old, she has been a gigantic inspiration to so many because of her selfless acts and ability to entertain others. Oprah Winfrey is an actress, director, producer, journalist, and a philanthropist. She has made such a positive impact on the world with her success story and what she's managed to accomplish and do for others. Because of all her success, she now owns her own network called The Oprah Winfrey Network (OWN). One of my favorite quotes is from Oprah. She says, "Don't worry about being successful, but work toward being significant, and the success will follow." I love this because being significant to others is living a life of purpose with positive impact. It's really not about all of the things we can accomplish for ourselves; it's about making sure that we can accomplish things so we can help others. All of us spiritual beings on this planet are partners in co-creation. If we accept and appreciate the diversity of all of the different desires and beliefs, all of us would have a much more expansive, rewarding, and gratifying experience.

CAMP REFLECTIONS

What are some ways that you are making a positive impact in the lives of others?

_____

_____

_____

_____

_____

_____

_____

_____

_____

_____

_____

_____

_____

_____

_____

_____

_____

_____

_____

_____

_____

PURPOSE OF POSITIVE IMPACT

What if everyone in the world was selfish and kept all of their money, talents, and resources to themselves? How would we expand and grow? We were born to co-create with each other and for each other. True success is not defined by how much money you make; it's defined by the positive impact you have on others. Making a positive impact in someone else's life doesn't take much; it just takes a willing heart to enrich the lives of others. A positive impact stems from our positive thinking, which comes from a positive attitude. We all have a personal responsibility to make a positive impact on society. It all starts with gratitude when we wake up in the morning. Gratitude leads to grace. I'm so grateful when I get the opportunity to have another shot at this life experience. When we are grateful and happy we naturally set ourselves up to have positive impact on others. Energy is powerful and when we are grateful and happy, we spread that positive infectious energy.

Helen Keller once said, "True happiness is not attained through self-gratification but through fidelity to a worthy purpose." Knowing that you can make a difference promotes a strong sense of self-worth and belief. I spent most of my adult life struggling financially, and for the longest time I felt insecure about my financial situation. I felt like I wasn't succeeding in life because I owed people money, I wasn't able to pay my bills on time consistently, my credit score was low, I had to tell my daughters "no" often, and that led to a bunch of "I can'ts" and insecurities. Normally this would really make one feel less than, but I knew not to have that mindset. Life is not about how much money we have; it's about who we are and how we live. It doesn't take money to make someone else's life better. It just takes effort, and I love seeing other people happy. There are so many lives that I have impacted simply by caring. Life is a gift, so it's important to stay present. Many people are suffering and in need of someone who cares. Let that be you—you be the person who makes a difference.

You don't need to do anything that doesn't come naturally for you in order to engage with someone and make a positive impact. Community leaders, teachers, coaches, entrepreneurs, parents, friends, and even strangers are all different ways to impact others. When we are warm, open and caring we have direct impact and it has a positive influence on ourselves and others. People who impact the world for the better know that they aren't perfect. They are students of life and will constantly work to grow in order to have the opportunity to gain more knowledge and resources. The more we grow the bigger the opportunity to make more positive impact. Your life has purpose. Your story is important. Your dreams count. Your voice matters. You were born to make an impact.

CAMP REFLECTIONS

Do you know what the purpose of your life is? Do you feel like your life has an impact on others? Write down three things that you absolutely love and feel like you were born to do. (They are probably tied into your purpose.)

_____

_____

_____

_____

_____

_____

_____

_____

_____

_____

_____

_____

_____

_____

_____

_____

_____

_____

_____

HOW TO MAKE A POSITIVE IMPACT

Every day that we wake up we have the chance to perform random acts of kindness that can positively impact the lives of others. It all starts first thing in the morning with gratitude when you open your eyes. That grateful energy that you put into the universe first thing in the morning could carry you through your day. So be very deliberate about having an amazing day each morning when you wake up. Remember that it all starts with gratitude because you woke up and that is a Blessing. Here are some simple ways to make a positive impact in the world:

1. **Spend Time with Loved Ones -** It is essential to spend time with the people that you love. Life gets extremely busy and challenging at times, but we can't forget to make time for the people we love. Our presence and love with the people we love goes a long way. We make a positive impact by simply being present with the people in our lives.

2. **Become the Best Version of You -** When we are constantly working on being the best version of ourselves, we have no choice but to have positive impact on others. People don't listen to what we say, they watch what we do. I noticed that when I truly started consistently keeping my mind, body, and spirit right; my close friends and families became inspired to do the same. When we are being the best versions of ourselves; it inspires people to be the best versions of themselves.

3. **Crack a Smile -** Did you know that when you smile you make life more beautiful? There are people suffering in this world, and you have the power to make them feel better just by smiling. Your smile can help people understand and believe that everything is going to be alright. Use your smile to positively impact

the world; don't let the world change your smile. Smiles are contagious, so spread smiles.

4. **Be Helpful to Others** - Being helpful to others can happen on a broad spectrum. it comes down to all of the little thoughtful things we do for each other to show that we care. When we help others, it gives a sense of meaning, connection, and purpose. Search for ways to be a blessing in someone else's life. Our willingness to help others is how we co-create together here during this human experience.

5. **Express Your Gratitude** - There are so many ways that you can show people that you are grateful for them. You can simply say, "thank you," when anyone does anything for you. Sending a thank you note is always a great way to show someone that you're grateful for them. You can also contact the people in your life who have inspired you, and let them know what they did for you, and what it means to you.

6. **Find Your Own Joy** - When we truly have joy in our own lives we put joy into the universe. The joy that we feel puts out so much positive energy into the universe; it has the ability to bring joy into other peoples' lives. So do the things that make you feel good, because as a great friend of mine, actor Raymond Barry once told me, "when you focus yourself into feeling good, life becomes delicious." Mother Teresa once said, "Joy is a net of love by which you can catch souls."

CAMP REFLECTIONS

How do you think you will be even more intentional going forward, consciously aware of the positive impact you can have on others?

_____

_____

_____

_____

_____

_____

_____

_____

_____

_____

_____

_____

_____

_____

_____

_____

_____

_____

EXAMPLE OF POSITIVE IMPACT

Waking Up with the Right Mindset set off a wave of positive impact the moment the book became available. The positive impact that it initially made on my daughters was the most gratifying for me. They witnessed the entire process of me writing and completing the book. So when I signed a book for each of them and gave it to them, it planted a powerful seed. It taught them that they could do and have whatever they want in life, if they believed in themselves, didn't doubt, and did the work. I understood how growing up watching family members shoot down my grandmother's dreams, ultimately made a negative impact on her life. As a result, I have been much more conscious about the seeds I plant in my daughters' lives. People don't listen to what you say, they watch what you do.

Completing the book made a positive impact in my own life as well. It boosted my self-esteem and self-confidence. It increased my faith and made me believe in and understand the universal laws even more. I understand the Law of Attraction with an even greater depth. I'm now truly aware, because of this experience, that thoughts turn into things in the absence of resistance. When we understand how these laws works, it makes it a lot easier to navigate through life. You understand that you are the creator of your own reality. So why not make positive impact while you're here during this human experience?

Since the book came out, I have been receiving a plethora of calls and messages from people who have read the book. I love the fact that the book is helping people change their perspective, which in turn, is helping them change their realities. The book has been promoting a positive mindset. One of my great friends Jerry, turned the book into a curriculum for his students. He understood the importance of supporting students with their emotional intelligence. The testimonials from his students alone have been beautiful.

Even during the writing process of this book, I had to incorporate the tools that I have in my belt. All of my financial matters haven't been solved, and the normal pressures of life still exist. I still have the right to panic if I'm allowing the absence of certain things, dictate who I am. However, it's living a life of CAMP that sustains us and makes us thrive during the journey of this life experience. Life is going to always cause us to want more and have new desires. That's why it's important to control your own alignment, so you can live a life of CAMP.

To be completely transparent, my goal is ultimately to have positive impact on everyone I encounter, whether it's cracking a smile, sharing a laugh, or helping someone see that they can change their perspective to have a happier life.

Imagine if I would've panicked when my investor told me that he was unable to fund my project last year in 2018? You wouldn't be reading this book. Remember that everything in life happens for a reason; there are no such things as coincidences. This is why you have to make it a habit to always trying to live a life of CAMP.

Positive Impact!

CAMP REFLECTIONS

Who are some people who have positively impacted your life? How did they positively impact your life?

MY WISH FOR YOU

My goal is ultimately to have a positive impact on everyone I encounter, whether it's cracking a smile, sharing a laugh, or helping someone see that they can change their perspective to have a happier life. My hopes and prayers are for you is to realize your purpose, and work to become the best version of yourself. Tomorrow isn't promised to any of us, but it is delicious knowing that you are living a life of CAMP.

Made in the USA
San Bernardino, CA
16 July 2020